SUCCESSFUL SELF-PUBLISHING

HOW TO SELF-PUBLISH AND MARKET YOUR
BOOK IN EBOOK, PRINT AND AUDIOBOOK
FORMATS

JOANNA PENN

CURL UP
PRESS

INTRODUCTION

This little book will give you an overview of the process to successfully self-publish.

It provides the exact way that I have used to self-publish over 30 books of fiction and non-fiction, and which provides the basis of my own multi-six-figure income as an author-entrepreneur.

But, of course, it wasn't always like this!

I self-published my first book in 2008 before ebooks went mainstream and people started to read on their phones, before the Kindle and print-on-demand and the rise of digital audiobooks. I made a lot of mistakes, but over time, I've learned the most effective way to self-publish in order to satisfy my own creativity *and* make a good income. I'll share it all with you so you can save time, money and heartache on your own author journey.

The book includes everything you need to self-publish in ebook, print, and audiobook formats, as well as details on how much it might cost and how you will get paid, plus tips on how to market fiction and non-fiction books.

Like any new process, it might seem complicated at first, but then it gets easier. Once you know how to publish in each of these formats, you will realize that *publishing* is not the hard part. Publishing a book takes just a couple of hours, but writing, editing, and marketing remain the most challenging aspects of the process!

This book represents my own self-publishing experience and opinions but, of course, I'm an indie (independent) author and we all vary in the way we approach publishing. That's the beauty of being independent — there are no rules! I've tried to ensure the information is accurate, but technology, functionality, and terms and conditions change over time, so please check the platform details when you publish.

Note: There are affiliate links within this book to products and services that I recommend and use personally. This means that I receive a small percentage of sales with no extra cost to you and in some cases, you may receive a discount for using my links. I only recommend products and services that I believe are great for authors!

INDIE AUTHOR VS. SELF-PUBLISHING

Before we jump into *how* to self-publish, it's important to define some terms at the outset.

S elf-publishing used to be a dirty word, with implications of 'vanity' publishing by authors so desperate that they would pay to have their book released into the world.

But these days, self-publishing is a valid choice and publishers regularly seek out successful authors who do well through the indie route. Some traditionally published authors also choose to self-publish some of their books in order to make the most of their options.

I consciously chose to self-publish back in 2008. I wanted to spend my time writing, creating books and running my own business, reaching readers directly in a growing global market and making a decent living. This is now what I do every day and it continues to fire my passion for the indie life.

Self-publishing is still the term used by most people, but

I prefer being described as an **independent** or **indie author**, or even as an author-entrepreneur.

Here are the differences between the terms in my opinion, and to be clear, there is no value judgment implied in the split definition. It's more about what you want to achieve as an author, and, of course, this may change over time.

A self-published author:

- Does everything themselves e.g. cover design and editing.
- Defines success as a finished book that is out there in the world and doesn't necessarily aim to sell a lot of books to readers.

This term is appropriate for creative projects with a lot of heart and potentially little commercial value e.g. I helped my 9-year-old niece self-publish her first book, as well as helping my 65-year-old father self-publish his thriller, *Nada*.

> Here's a video that Amazon made about us for Father's Day:
> www.TheCreativePenn.com/fathersday

Neither of these projects were commercial, as both saw the completion of the book as the end goal, not the sales associated with it.

An indie (independent) author:

- Budgets for and works with creative professionals to make their book into a fantastic finished product. This may include working with editors and cover designers, as well as formatters and other freelancers.

- Understands that a book is an intellectual property asset that can earn money for the life of the author and 50-70 years after they die.
- Defines success as long-term income as well as creative fulfilment.
- Takes control of their writing career, from first book to (potentially) CEO of a global creative empire.

Here are the main reasons that authors choose to go indie.

Empowerment and creative control

You don't need to ask anyone's permission to write or publish. You can write whatever you want and publish whenever you want. You have control over your book title, your cover, and your pricing. You also have control over the territories that you publish in, for example, I have now sold books in 86 countries.

Speed

You can publish a book and have it available for sale in less than 24 hours (for ebooks), then receive payment just a few months later. Print books can be available for sale in a few days and audiobooks in a few weeks.

For authors used to the year-long traditional publishing cycle, this speed is incredibly rewarding.

Scalable income

If you self-publish, you receive 35-70% royalty on the sale of ebooks, which is better than pretty much every traditional publishing deal out there. If you sell direct from your own site, then you can get up to 90%. You can set your own profit margin on print books and you can get 25-40+% audiobook royalties.

Every book you write adds to your financial bottom line and you don't have to sell your time working to build someone else's business or brand. You can publish in every global market and license subsidiary rights, so your income is scalable on every book.

Transparency of sales and income

It's difficult for traditionally published authors to determine what kind of marketing works because they don't get real-time sales figures, whereas indies can check reports that are updated every few hours. This helps determine which marketing avenues to focus on for ongoing sales.

We can also track our income every day and reconcile it with our payments each month, whereas royalty statements from traditional publishers are notoriously hard to under-stand and reconcile.

But, of course, it's not all sunshine and roses!

Being an indie author means taking on the jobs that traditional agents and publishers do for their authors until you can build your own team of creative professionals.

Some authors don't actually want freedom, they would prefer that someone else did the publishing and marketing side and are happy to give up the lion's share of their royalty for that privilege.

Plus, just because your book is available everywhere, it doesn't mean that it will sell.

So, if you want to *successfully* self-publish, you will have to **learn new skills** around publishing and marketing. Yes, you will make mistakes along the way. We all do. But you can learn from them and do things differently with your next book.

I'm still learning, as we all are, but I enjoy all aspects of being an indie, not just the writing. This is a brilliant life, if it suits your personality.

If you're ready for the adventure, read on!

PART I

HOW TO SELF-PUBLISH

1.1 BEFORE YOU SELF-PUBLISH

In this chapter, I'll go through the prerequisites BEFORE you publish, regardless of format.

Along the way, I'll provide recommendations for various tools that I use, although of course, you will develop your own system over time.

(1) Write a great book!

This is not a 'how to write' book, but I'm assuming that you have written the best book possible and that you have used a professional editor and/or proofreader to make sure it is the best it can be.

If you need craft help, I have books on how to write fiction and non-fiction, as well as courses on those topics.

If you need a professional editor, check out
www.TheCreativePenn.com/editors

(2) Decide on your definition of success

Most authors write their first book because something is burning on their heart. They have a story to tell, a life experience to share, or they want to help people and change the world.

Essentially, that first book is all about you, the author.

And that's fine, all the way up to the point of publication.

But I get emails every day from authors who are disappointed with their sales, even though they haven't considered the reader up to that point. They wrote the book of their heart without considering the customer or the potential market. Sales hadn't been a factor until the book was out.

If you want to be 'successful,' then define what 'success' means for you. Don't be disappointed later on. Here are some possibilities:

- You want to hold your book in your hand and say, 'I made this!'
- You want to win a literary prize and receive critical acclaim
- You want your book on the shelves in your local bookstore so your family and friends can be proud
- You want to make a full-time living with your writing

These are all great definitions, but the truth is that some of these are mutually exclusive.

Would you rather win a literary prize or make a million dollars?

Over and above just finishing a book, there are two extreme ends of the author success scale.

At one end is E.L. James with *Fifty Shades of Grey,* who made $95 million in a single year with book deals, movies and all kinds of exciting things. Not many people would say that *Fifty Shades* is great literature — but readers love the books and it sure is making a living!

At the other end is wanting to win a literary prize where the aim is critical acclaim and awards rather than money. Most literary authors have other jobs and don't earn as much as genre fiction authors.

You have to consider the two extremes for yourself: literary success, critical acclaim, and validation vs. commercial success, a healthy bank balance and millions of happy readers.

There is no value judgment either way. It's really about considering what's important to you and about how you're going to measure your own success.

If you don't decide in advance, how will you know when you have hit your goal? I've found that the most disappointed authors are the ones who thought they wanted one thing but actually craved something else. So, be honest. It's your author journey.

(3) Get a great cover design

Book covers and visual images are increasingly important in a crowded market. A professional book cover is critical for the publishing process, but it's also a key part of your marketing.

Research the bestselling books in your genre and note the common elements of design and imagery. For example, George R. R. Martin's *Game of Thrones* books have dragons, crowns, and swords, so anything with similar imagery is likely to be fantasy or historical fiction.

Non-fiction books often have a big focus on text and font, which makes them stand out at thumbnail size on the bookstore sites. There are conventions in every genre, so get to know yours.

Take screen-prints of book covers that you like and send them to your designer along with your book description.

> [Note: This is about modeling, not plagiarism. Your designer should never copy a cover, but design something appropriate for your genre.]

You can have covers for each format designed separately, but you are likely to get a better deal if you get them all at the same time. The print cover needs a spine and back cover, whereas the ebook version only needs a front cover, and the audiobook cover is square, so needs to be reformatted into new dimensions.

The ebook and audiobook covers should be optimised for the thumbnail size image that is displayed on the retail stores and phone screens, but you can always add extra text on the print cover if that is important to you e.g. blurb from an author in your genre or a particularly good review quote.

One of the benefits of being an indie author is that you can always replace the cover, so it's not a disaster if you end up changing it later. If you want to revamp things or re-launch, then changing covers is one of the best ways you can do this. Traditional publishers do this all the time, and I've changed my own covers and even titles over time. Never be afraid to redo your covers if you think that it will help sell the book better.

Don't make your own book covers unless you are a book cover designer.

> There are specific skills around image design, so check out this list: www.TheCreativePenn.com/bookcoverdesign to find someone suitable or ask other indie authors who they use.

If you really don't have the budget, then have a look at the free covers on Canva.com.

(4) Write your sales description

It's hard to write a book, but sometimes it's harder to distill that book into a couple of paragraphs for the sales description and back cover. However, you do need to do it or hire someone who can help you.

Think about your own behavior as a reader. You check out the cover and then you read the description. You make a purchasing decision based on those few short lines.

So, your description is crucial, as it can make the difference between someone downloading a sample, buying your book, or just ignoring it.

Again, you don't need to panic, as one of the great things about being an indie author is the ability to change things, so you can update your sales description over time.

A great way to start is to model successful books in your genre.

Go to the bestseller lists in your category and copy out the top ten blurbs from those books. By copying them out you will quickly grasp the 'formula' of the genre, whether it is crime fiction, entrepreneurship or children's books. Once again, I'm talking about modeling here, not plagiarism!

For fiction, this includes hyperbole about the plot, aspects of the key character and often their name, a hook to the plot and a call to action.

For non-fiction, focus on solving the problem that the reader has and hook them in to wanting more. You can also list your table of contents if that will help, plus information about your expertise and your own story, so it's clear that you're an authority in this area.

You could also include review quotes from other authors or media and an interview with the author.

If you need help with sales descriptions, check out the following books:

- *Gotta Read It! 5 Simple Steps to a Fiction Pitch that Sells* by Libbie Hawker
- *How to Write a Sizzling Synopsis: A Step-by-Step System for Enticing New Readers, Selling More Fiction, and Making Your Books Sound Good* by Bryan Cohen

You will need to copy and paste your book description into the self-publishing platforms later on using plain text or formatted HTML.

I use a formatting tool from Kindlepreneur which enables me to display the headline at a different font size and use italics, spacing and bullet points.

You can find it at TheCreativePenn.com/rocketdescription

(5) Decide on your categories and keywords

Metadata is the information that the book sales sites use to categorize your book, and they use it in the algorithms that help with book recommendation.

Metadata is super-important for ensuring that readers can find your book and includes:

- Title and sub-title
- Series title
- Sales description
- Categories
- Keywords
- Author bio

As 'big data' becomes more prevalent, it's likely that even the text of your book will eventually be used as metadata. Again, being indie is an advantage, as we can change these fields over time and react to shifts in the market.

Categories and keywords, in particular, are important in terms of book discovery

Categories are used on all ebook platforms and you can usually choose between two and five. On print and audio-book platforms, this is usually the BISAC code. The aim is to be granular enough that your book can stand out but not so deep down the hierarchy that no one shops there.

For example, there's absolutely no point in putting your novel in Fiction/General, as people just won't be able to find it. Readers tend to shop in sub-categories, so this is where you need to put your book.

Research which categories other authors/books similar

to yours are using. For *Stone of Fire*, I chose the two categories Action Adventure and Supernatural Thrillers.

You can also get into more categories by using 'browse categories' through keywords on Amazon. For example, I use Conspiracy Thriller as a keyword, which gets my book into the Conspiracy Thriller category on Amazon.

If you need help deciding on sub-categories to target on Amazon, check out the reports on K-lytics:
www.TheCreativePenn.com/genre

You can also use Publisher Rocket to identify categories and keywords:
www.TheCreativePenn.com/rocket

You can also check out my tutorial on how to use Publisher Rocket:
www.TheCreativePenn.com/rocket-tutorial

Keywords, or keyword phrases, are a separate metadata field on the publishing platforms, and you can usually select up to seven.

How do you decide on keywords?

You can use the Amazon search bar to discover the words and phrases that people are searching for. Just start typing in the box and you will get a dropdown that auto-populates based on the most popular searches. Spend some time trying different combinations and you'll be amazed at what you find.

You can also use popular keyword research tool, Publisher Rocket to automate this:
www.TheCreativePenn.com/rocket

You can also check out my tutorial on how to use Publisher Rocket:
www.TheCreativePenn.com/rocket-tutorial

The principle is the same for fiction and non-fiction, but for non-fiction it's even better because you can title your book to match the keywords that people search for.

My first book was originally called *How To Love Your Job or Find a New One*. After discovering keywords, I changed my title to *Career Change* and the book began to sell more since people were actually searching for 'career change' on Amazon, whereas they weren't searching for the original title.

1.2 WHY SELF-PUBLISH AN EBOOK?

Many readers are still emotionally attached to print, and we'll come onto self-publishing print later on, but I still meet many authors who have not self-published an ebook version of their book. If you're one of those who are still on the fence, I'll explain why this is so critical.

Most indie authors make the majority of their income from ebooks.

There's more profit per ebook because there's no printing or shipping. Readers can buy immediately they hear about the book, so the barrier to purchase is lower and marketing is easier.

You can sell your books to anyone in the world over the internet. You can compete on a level playing field with any other book in the world, whereas most indies struggle to get their work into physical bookstores.

You really can have a multinational global business from your writing desk. Exciting!

Many people also prefer reading ebook editions. For example, I only read fiction in ebook now. If you don't have an ebook version of your book, you're missing out on a chunk of revenue and readership.

Ebooks are a huge growth market globally

There are reports in the traditional press about the slowing down of ebook sales in the US and UK. But this is skewed by data that only report on books with ISBNs and miss out the growing number of readers who consume books through subscription services like KDP Select and Scribd which use 'borrows' instead of purchases.

Many indies, myself included, don't use ISBNs for ebooks so our sales aren't included in traditional media reports anyway.

The ebook market is considered 'mature' in the US, UK, Canada, and Australia, but most of the rest of the world has barely started. Several years ago, I had only sold books in five countries but now I've sold books (in English) in 86 countries.

Those global sales streams are trickles right now, but they will only grow as readers start to transition to digital. It's inevitable with the rise of mobile technology and streaming internet.

The speed of publishing means you have control of when and how readers can get your book

Once you click Publish, your ebook can be for sale within 24 hours, sometimes it's up in less than 4 hours. So, you can publish and have a book earning you money before lunch. That's just brilliant!

Ebooks are lower risk because they have a lower cost of entry

It is free to self-publish on the most popular ebook platforms.

Obviously, you have to pay upfront for editing and cover design, but the actual publishing is free, and the stores take a small percentage of sales. Compared to most other business models, publishing in this digital age has low overheads, low entry cost and potentially a high margin of return.

But what about piracy?

I always get asked about piracy when I speak about ebooks. There are a few things to consider.

Most readers are not pirates.

Most readers are wonderful people who are happy to support authors. Why miss out on the huge potential for fear of the pirates?

Piracy will happen anyway if your book is popular.

There's really no way of stopping piracy, but what do you think the most pirated books are? Harry Potter and other big sellers, of course. Not the unknowns.

Most people who pirate books are not going to be your readers anyway. It's more important to consider obscurity than piracy. More authors suffer from being completely unknown than from being famous enough to be significantly pirated.

Some authors have used piracy as a marketing tool.

Paulo Coelho, author of *The Alchemist*, released his book in Russia on the pirate sites and his sales picked up after word spread about him. Self-help author, Tim Ferriss, launched *The 4 Hour Chef* with a promotion on Bit Torrent which resulted in massive sales.

Stay aware just in case.

You can set up alerts with sites like mention.net around your book title or lines from your book. There are ways to get your books taken down, but in my experience, they pop up again all over the place, sometimes on phishing sites that want you to click on links.

If you are seriously worried, then check out *The Self-Publisher's Legal Handbook* by Helen Sedwick, which offers some options.

1.3 HOW TO FORMAT AN EBOOK

Hopefully, you're now convinced that you need to publish an ebook. So, how do you get started?

You need a formatted ebook file to load to the publishing platforms. This is your completed, edited manuscript in specific formats: mobi for Amazon and ePub for the other stores.

You have two options to produce these:

(1) Learn how to **do it yourself** – as I do. It really isn't that hard, especially if you have plain text books without tables and images. There are also many software options to help you nowadays.

(2) Outsource this task and **pay a professional** to format your book.

Why learn to do it yourself?

One of the reasons I like to keep formatting in my control is because we often change our ebooks over time.

Every time I put out a new book in a series, I want to

update the back matter of the previous books with links to the new book.

There are also the inevitable typos. Even if you use multiple proofreaders, someone will always find a problem later. It may be within a month or two, it may be a year later, and you know you're going to want to fix it! If you have control, you can fix it yourself and upload a new file easily for no extra cost.

If you outsource this task, you will need to pay for these updates, and it won't be as fast.

Do-it-yourself formatting

I use Scrivener as my writing tool, and Vellum as my publishing tool.

Vellum is Mac-only, but many authors buy a second-hand Mac in order to use it because it makes formatting easy and fun. You can also use Mac-In-Cloud from a PC.

Check Vellum software out at:
www.TheCreativePenn.com/vellum

You can also find my tutorial on how to use it at:
www.TheCreativePenn.com/vellum-tutorial

There are other options for doing it yourself.

- Draft2Digital have a formatting tool
- Reedsy have a writing and formatting tool
- Amazon KDP have Kindle Create, a Kindle only formatting tool

Also, if you have books in print from previous

publishing deals, you can get them scanned from print back into Word so you can produce an ebook from that retrospectively.

Many authors who had deals over ten years ago will own their ebook rights, so it's worth checking your contracts to see if you can publish digital versions, even if a traditional publisher owns your print rights. You might have only licensed a specific territory e.g. US and Canada, so you could self-publish in other global markets.

Considerations for images

If you have a lot of images in your book or a lot of complicated tables, then you will have some problems in ebook formatting. You will also have a bigger file size. Although ebooks are typically free in terms of delivery, Amazon does include a delivery cost in their pricing setup which will be higher if you have a bigger file and images really expand the file size. If your delivery cost goes too high, you're not going to make much royalty. So, it's important to consider the size of your file and whether you really need those images.

If you write children's books, consider the Kindle Kids Book Creator, which is a specific tool for image-heavy children's books. You can also check out iBooks Author, which can be used for children's books on the iPad as well as textbooks with enhanced video and images.

Amazon has other tools for image-heavy books, including Kindle Edu for enhanced textbooks and Kindle Comic Creator for comics and graphic novels.

If you're writing non-fiction with images, consider whether you really need them and whether they are critical to the reader's experience.

Authors can get romantically attached to images that

actually might not be needed. It might be better to put your images on your website and include links within your ebooks. This will get people over to your website, where they could potentially sign up for your email list. You could also put the images on a Pinterest board for social media sharing and use them for marketing. You could also consider using images in your print book but not in the ebook or (obviously) the audiobook versions.

The other thing to consider with images is ensuring you have the right copyright license. Are they your own images? Do you have permission to use them and what type of license have you paid for?

Outsource ebook formatting

If you want to outsource formatting, then check out this **list of formatting options and professionals:** www.TheCreativePenn.com/formatting

1.4 EXCLUSIVITY AND GOING DIRECT

Before you publish, you need to make a couple of decisions that impact the stores your ebook will sell on.

(1) Do you want to publish on multiple platforms or go exclusive with Amazon?

You can publish on Amazon KDP as well as all the other platforms, but Amazon also offers KDP Select, which is a specific service that you can opt into for 90-day periods.

If you opt-in, your ebook will be included in Kindle Unlimited (KU), a subscription service where books are more likely to be borrowed by readers who pay a fixed price per month instead of buying books individually.

There are other advantages around free promotion days or countdown deals as well as visibility in the store. You are paid based on pages read from a pot of money shared between authors at the end of each month. This amount changes every month and is determined by Amazon.

If you only have one book and are just starting out, then

it's definitely worth using KDP Select at least for the first 90 days. Or, if you have several books in unrelated niches, then it's also potentially worth doing.

Some authors choose to build their entire business on Amazon, using KDP Select as their primary income source but if you have multiple books in a series and you want to make a living with your writing for the long term, then going wide to other platforms is the best idea, in my opinion. You'll reach more readers in different markets and build a more diverse and resilient eco-system for your books. You won't be subject to the many changes that impact KDP Select authors and you won't have to worry about being targeted by scammers who focus on the KU market.

Of course, it takes time to grow your audience at other stores and having multiple books in a series as well as boxsets can be the best way to gain reader loyalty and sales for the long term.

Remember, KDP Select is for ebooks only, so even if you choose to go exclusive with Amazon for your ebook, you can still go 'wide' with your print book and audiobook. This way, you can still reach libraries and bookstores with your words rather than being locked inside the Amazon eco-system. After all, we are *independent* authors, aren't we?!

(2) If going wide, do you want to go direct to the platforms and/or use an aggregator?

There are hundreds of sites that sell ebooks across the world right now and there is no way to individually publish to them all. Plus, you want to spend your time writing, not updating multiple publishing sites.

Luckily, there are aggregators who will publish your

books to multiple vendors while taking a small percentage of sales in return.

I publish direct to Amazon KDP, Apple Books, and Kobo Writing Life because I want to retain control of my biggest income sources as well as take advantage of their promotions.

I use aggregator services Draft2Digital for Nook and library sites, and PublishDrive for Google Play and other sites.

I also sell direct to my readers through

www.CreativePennBooks.com which gives me the most control and the highest royalties (over 90% for digital products).

I've been independently publishing for over a decade now, so I have added new services as they have emerged in order to reach more markets. I am totally committed to wide distribution and having my books available everywhere, but I'll admit that it takes time to manage updates on all my books on all these different platforms every time I want to make a change.

You have to decide what works best for your book and your own publishing process over time.

1.5 HOW TO SELF-PUBLISH AN EBOOK

T he main sites for direct self-publishing are Amazon KDP, Kobo Writing Life, Barnes and Noble Press, and iTunes Connect for Apple Books. The main ebook aggregators are Draft2Digital (which acquired Smashwords in 2022), PublishDrive, and StreetLib.

Each of the platforms has a similar set of fields, even if their look and feel is slightly different.

It's important to note that none of the platforms require programming or any kind of technical ability. If you can use Google and MS Word, you can self-publish an ebook!

The best way to learn is to set up an account on the various stores and have a go. If you have all the relevant information ready, it shouldn't take too long to get your book out into the world. Exciting!

In this section, I will briefly outline the information you will need.

Book Title

You need to enter the exact title as shown on your cover. This is because people used to 'stuff' keywords into the title field e.g. "Paranormal romance with a noir detective twist." If it's not on the cover, you can't include it here!

You can change your title if you want to rebrand the books later.

Sub-title

Optional. Often used for non-fiction books, the sub-title may contain some of the keywords discussed earlier.

Series title and volume

Books in a series are often linked together on the online stores and customers are notified at the end of one book about the others in the series. You can also use series for non-fiction in order to group books for a similar audience.

Edition number

If you substantially update a book over time, you can use different edition numbers.

Publisher

Optional. This can be your company name or an imprint name that you decide on, or you can just leave it blank. After all, readers don't generally shop by publisher.

You don't need an imprint or a company to self-publish,

but it's something to consider later if you turn your writing into a business.

Description

This is the sales description or the back blurb, as described in the previous section.

Book contributors

This is your author name, which may or may not be your real name. I publish under Joanna Penn for non-fiction and J.F.Penn for fiction. You can also add co-authors, translators, editors and other parties here if you want to credit them.

Language

As a reader of this book, I assume that most of your books will be in English, but I have self-published books in French, German, Italian and Spanish. Indies are moving into translation as new markets open up, plus many authors are now self-publishing from other countries. The indie movement is growing!

ISBN

Optional. You don't need to use an ISBN for your ebook as all of the sites have options to use free ones or Amazon uses their own ASIN for Kindle books. If you do have your own ISBNs, you can enter one here.

For more detail on ISBN, check out this article from the Alliance of Independent Authors: www.TheCreativePenn.com/isbn

Verify your publishing rights

Public domain books are out of copyright. So, say you wanted to publish *Frankenstein* by Mary Shelley, you could publish it but it's likely that one of the official versions would sell better and it's available for free everywhere anyway.

For your own books, select "This is not a public domain work and I hold the necessary publishing rights."

Categories

As covered in chapter 1.1, you should already have done your research and chosen the appropriate categories. Now you just need to add them here.

For Amazon, you get two choices, Kobo allows three and Apple Books allows more, as does Draft2Digital.

Age range

Optional. This is mainly for children's books, which are becoming more popular in digital format.

Keywords

As per chapter 1.1, you should have done your research on the type of thing that your customers search for and then enter them here.

Book release option

Do you want to publish now or have the book up for pre-order?

Pre-orders are especially good for books in a series, as readers are often ready to order the next one as soon as they finish the one before. You can set them up to a year in advance on Apple Books and Kobo and three months on Amazon. On Apple Books, you get sales rankings for the pre-order period and for the actual sales day, so it's well worth doing it there. For Amazon, you spread your sales over the pre-order period, so you'll need to weigh up what's best for your book.

If you don't want to do a pre-order, just select "I am ready to release my book now."

Book cover

Upload your high-resolution book cover design. You can always replace this later if you want to rebrand.

Upload your book file

This is mobi for Kindle or ePub for other stores.

If it works, the upload will be shown as successful. You may get a notification of errors or spelling mistakes. Just fix them and re-upload another file if you need to.

Most indies upload new files periodically to update back matter. This is why control of your own formatting is so useful.

DRM

Digital Rights Management is a way of locking a book to a specific format.

I don't enable digital rights management on any platform. As far as I'm concerned, if readers want to read my book on another device, they should be able to. So, I always click, "Do not enable digital rights management." It's your choice.

Preview your book

Most of the publishing platforms offer a way to preview your book file as the customer will see it. Amazon's preview tool offers a view per device, e.g. Kindle Fire vs. iPhone, which is great, especially if you have specific formatting/tables/images.

If there are problems, no worries. Just fix the file and re-upload.

If you're going to self-publish ebooks or you are already selling them, then I recommend that you buy an ebook reader or at least try reading an ebook on one of the many free apps on your phone or tablet. You need to understand the mindset of an ebook reader as well as their online experience.

I read ebooks on the Kindle Paperwhite and my iPhone Kindle app. I mostly download samples before buying, unless I know and trust the author when I will often pre-order the ebook when I hear about it. I also have preferences around pricing, and you will pick these things up if you try reading digitally.

Verify your publishing territories

If you are self-publishing and you hold all the rights, just click, "Worldwide."

If you are traditionally published, you may own rights in other territories. For example, say you published with a publisher in the US and sold only the US rights, you could self-publish in the UK or Australia or any other country. You can select individual territories and deselect the ones that you have licensed to someone else.

Set your pricing

Most of the stores have country-specific pricing and it's well worth setting these individually instead of relying on an automatic exchange rate calculation.

For example, if you price at US$4.99 and just leave it to automatically calculate for GBP, then readers in the UK might see £3.21, which is an odd price.

It's best to change the UK price to £2.99 or £3.49 which is a price that readers are more used to seeing. Amazon has specific price bands for royalties, so you need to price between US$2.99 and $9.99 if you want 70% royalty. If you're pricing below or above that, then it's 35%. Other stores do not have these restrictions.

Kindle MatchBook

Amazon-specific field. If the print book is available and the customer has already bought it, they can get the eBook at a reduced price. I always select this.

Kindle Book Lending

Amazon-specific field that allows readers to lend books to friends and family in specific territories, which I think is a good thing, so I always select this too.

Click Save and Publish

The ebook will go through processing and within 4-24 hours, it will appear on the online bookstores. Super exciting!

A few more thoughts on pricing

New authors often agonize over pricing, so here are some tips:

You can **change the price anytime,** so start with something and change it later if it's not working for you.

Consider the value to the customer and what they can get for that price within the same genre.

For example, if John Grisham's latest legal thriller is $4.99, you can't really price your first legal thriller at $9.99. I have fiction at free, $2.99 for novellas, $4.99 for full-length novels, $6.99-$8.99 for boxsets, $7.99-$9.99 for non-fiction and higher prices for other items.

The more books you have, the more flexibility you have with pricing, and you won't be so emotionally attached to any individual book.

It's hard to put up a book for free if it's your only one, but when you have multiple books in a series, it's not hard at all to put the first at permanently free (permafree) as many authors do. If readers enjoy that, they might consider buying the rest of the series.

Free is a marketing strategy, in the same way that offering samples of cheese or wine in shops helps people to discover new tastes, so they might go on to buy the rest of the product.

It's very useful when you have a series, as it can lead people into buying the rest of the books. If you want to make a book permafree, then you need to price it for $0 on other stores e.g. Kobo, Draft2Digital, PublishDrive, and then report the lower price to Amazon so they will price match it to $0.

Kobo and Apple Books both have the capability to **schedule pricing promotions** so you can set and forget, and the price will revert after a discount period.

KDP Select does have some price scheduling tools, but if you're not exclusive with Amazon, you have to change it to the discount price and then go back in and change it back after the discount period is over.

A word on EU VAT tax:

In Dec 2014, a law was brought in across the EU that meant sales of digital products, including ebooks, would now be subject to Value Added Tax based on the country of the *customer*, not the supplier.

The law was aimed at stopping companies like Amazon, Google and Apple from situating their companies in countries with specific tax breaks to lower their tax in other countries. But of course, it hit every author and small business selling digitally. This tax is now spreading to other countries, so we can assume it will be part of the global digital marketplace going forward.

It affects you because this tax is now included in your list price so you will be paid less per book, but all the technical stuff is handled by the distributor, so you don't need to worry about doing it yourself.

If you want to sell direct from your own website, you can use PayHip or other services that handle EU digital VAT for you, or you can use a Shopify store which has apps to help.

1.6 WHY SELF-PUBLISH A PRINT BOOK?

This is easy: we love books!

I'm a biblioholic and if you're like me, you spend lots of money on books and they feature in your everyday life as escape, entertainment, learning, and pleasure. I grew up devouring books in the library and asked for books most birthdays. I go to my local bookstore several times a week and buy books almost daily online.

The physical book likely holds a powerful sway over you, so you should publish a print book for the joy of holding it in your hand and saying, "I made this!"

But you should also consider print from a business perspective because if you get emotional about it, you might find it will cost you a lot of money.

There are a number of good reasons to have a print book.

Many readers still prefer print books, so if you don't have one, then you're missing out on that market, especially in print-heavy genres like non-fiction, poetry, children's books and more.

They are useful for **marketing** and giveaways to readers. It's hard to send a signed copy of an ebook, although it can be done through Authorgraph.

They are great for **comparison pricing** on the online bookstores because it makes the ebook look like a great deal due to the perceived reduced price. For example, my book *Crypt of Bone* is $11.99 in paperback and $4.99 on Kindle, so the reader can save $7, or 63%. A bargain! I also have Large Print and hardback editions as well as an audiobook, so the reader has a lot of choice.

1.7 PRINT-ON-DEMAND WILL
CHANGE YOUR LIFE

I self-published my first book back in 2008. I was living in Australia and this was before the international Kindle, before ebooks and print-on-demand became mainstream. A print book was really the only option and so I did a short run with a local printer.

I paid a considerable amount of money to have 2000 books printed. I thought they would fly off the shelves, making me money and changing people's lives.

Despite being on national TV and radio, I only ended up selling around 100 books and I took the rest to the landfill, because later that year, I discovered ebooks, print-on-demand and internet marketing. I never looked back. So, now I'm passionate about helping others avoid my own expensive mistake!

What is print-on-demand (POD)?

You load a cover file and an interior book file to a POD service and when a customer orders one of your books from

Amazon, Barnes & Noble or another online bookstore, ONE copy is printed and sent directly to the customer.

This has incredible benefits:

- No upfront printing costs
- No warehousing or inventory management or accounting for stock
- No piles of books in your garage
- No shipping costs, packaging or running down to the post office every day to manage delivery
- No pulping of leftover books and no remainders going to the landfill

It's free to self-publish on many of the POD platforms, and they just take a cut of the sale.

You set the profit margin on the books, so you get paid later without having an outlay upfront.

You can also order multiple author copies or do bulk sales from POD sites like Ingram Spark, as well as include discounting and return options so bookstores, universities, schools and libraries can also order your books.

After my own terrible experience with doing a print run, I think print-on-demand is pretty amazing. When I teach this in live classes, people's eyes light up with the realization that publishing print books is achievable *without* spending thousands of dollars.

With Amazon Prime, you can even get your own books faster with POD than you can get traditional books, which have to come from a warehouse.

Create multiple formats

It's not just about doing a standard paperback anymore. I have paperbacks, Large Print Editions, Workbooks, and even Hardback editions for my books. All print-on-demand.

You can also get special paper, full-color and all kinds of other options now. These extras will impact the printing price, of course, but you get to choose what you want to create.

What about quality?

The criticism of POD books used to be their quality but if you order any of my print books, you'll find the quality is pretty much indistinguishable from those on bookstore shelves. Many publishers now use the same POD services that indie authors use.

I use an independent print on demand service for my store at www.CreativePennBooks.com and the quality is excellent.

When would you do a print run?

Of course, there are times when doing a print run can be a good option.

When the beauty of the finished product is important.

My friend and founder of the Alliance of Independent Authors, Orna Ross, did a hardback, gold-embossed, limited edition run of *Secret Rose*, a combination of WB Yeats *A Secret Rose* and Orna's own book, *Her Secret Rose*.

Orna did a crowd-funding campaign to raise the

printing costs and then sold the book at a premium. It was also a special project for Yeats' 150th anniversary, and there was a lot of work involved. So, this is something to do rarely, on special occasions.

I'd like to do a limited edition book one day where I make the paper and do the bookbinding myself. We can do these creative projects as indies, but they can't form the backbone of our author business, because the overheads in time and money are so high. But you can combine these special edition projects with POD to offer experiences at different levels to your fans.

If you have an established distribution method for your books.

Professional speakers have been self-publishing and selling books at the back of the room for years, and many make very good money that way.

If you have a physical business, e.g. you're a chiropractor or consultant or someone who has a place to sell and store books, then it may also work. But you have to be sure of your distribution channels, e.g. if you print 2000 books, you can sell them at 20 speaking events in the next six months.

If these reasons don't apply, then print-on-demand is definitely the way to go. And even if you do a print run, it's worth having a POD version as well, so you can distribute globally through online sites.

1.8 BEFORE YOU PRINT

S o, which print-on-demand (POD) company should you use?

There are four main self-service POD options and how you use them will depend on your goals for your print books.

KDP Print

This is Amazon's own print-on-demand service and is accessible through your Amazon KDP Dashboard at

kdp.amazon.com.

Authors used to print through Createspace, also owned by Amazon, but that service shut down in 2018 and the functionality rolled into KDP Print.

You can print in multiple sizes for paperback books and you can choose extended distribution if you want to have your book available to bookstores and libraries, although there is no discounting so it's less likely they will order through Amazon.

Ingram Spark

Ingram Spark has the widest printing and distribution options with partnerships with over 30,000 bookstores, universities, and retailers as well as the online stores.

They are also able to do hardbacks, embossing, flyleafs, and other special types of printing that other services don't offer.

Ingram Spark allows returns and offer discounting for retailers, so take that into account when you price your book. Personally, I don't do returns and I choose the lowest discount, as I prefer making money from my books rather than having to pay for distribution.

Ingram Spark does have some minor setup costs, but you can often find promo codes e.g. for NaNoWriMo, or if you're a member of the Alliance of Independent Authors, that will help you minimise your initial outlay.

My print sales have more than doubled since I started publishing with IngramSpark.

Blurb

Blurb have options for photo books and also have a direct to iPad publishing option, as well as a whole section for charities and also for children. When I helped my 9-year-old niece self-publish, we used Blurb as a non-commercial project.

Barnes and Noble Press

An amalgamated self-publishing service with both NOOK ebooks and POD for Barnes and Noble. Distribution is US only.

Drop-shipping print for direct sales

If you want to sell print direct to readers but you don't want to handle the shipping or keep books in your house, then you can use POD services like Lulu or Bookvault.app that integrate into online stores like Shopify or WooCommerce.

I use Bookvault with Shopify for my print books through www.CreativePennBooks.com.

Recommendation: Use KDP Print + Ingram Spark for the widest reach

KDP Print is a great service for selling print books on Amazon so you should definitely use that service.

However, KDP Print is an Amazon company and many bookstores won't stock books by Amazon. Barnes and Noble Press is only available in the USA and Blurb is more for personal projects. None of these services allow discounting, which is essential for bookstores.

So, if you want the widest distribution for your books, then the Alliance of Independent Authors recommends using KDP Print for Amazon only (so, don't select Extended Distribution) and then publish on Ingram Spark as well for access to bookstores, libraries and global stores.

This is the setup I now use for my own books as it gives me the widest distribution for print, plus the ability to do hardbacks which I love!

You need a few specific things for print-on-demand in addition to everything covered in section 1.1 Before you self-publish.

(1) Interior print file

This is your book in a print-ready format and there are options to do this yourself, or you can hire a professional to do it for you.

You'll need to decide on the size. I like 5x8 sizing for my books. I use cream paper for fiction and white for non-fiction, and my interiors are only black & white.

Try measuring some of the books on your bookshelf and see what feels 'right' in your hand. I like 5x8, as I can even use it for novellas around 28,000 words which look thin but are still worth doing.

For formatting the interior print file, you can get free templates on KDP Print and Ingram Spark and then just flow your text into them.

> You can also use Vellum for print formatting. Here's my tutorial:
>   www.TheCreativePenn.com/vellum-tutorial

There are various things that can go wrong with an interior file, as I discovered when I formatted my first book myself.

It needs to be consistent, with chapter headings, sub-headings and page numbering correctly formatted, with odd numbers on the right and certain pages blank with no page numbers.

You might also want to add visual elements like a motif at the beginning of each chapter to make the print book more attractive, as I do with my books.

Many authors enjoy this type of formatting, but personally, I prefer to hire a professional for print, although I do ebook formatting myself.

You can find formatting help at: www.TheCreativePenn.com/formatting

(2) Cover file

A cover for a print book includes the front, back and spine.

The spine size is calculated from the paper type and the number of pages, which in turn is based on the size of the book, which font and font size you use and other interior design decisions.

The back of the book usually has the sales description, your author bio and your author picture if you want to use one. Remember to include your website. There should also be space for the barcode, which is usually generated by the POD company.

Remember that you are publishing globally when you use POD, so don't include a price on your cover, since the book will sell in multiple currencies.

(3) ISBN

An ISBN, International Standard Book Number, is the number that the book industry has used for many years to identify books in their computer systems.

ISBNs are issued in each country by different companies, for example, Bowker in the US or Nielsen in the UK. The cost will vary as well, with some countries, like Canada, issuing them for free.

You do not have to use your own ISBNs in order to publish a book in any format, although the Alliance of Independent Authors does recommend that authors own their own ISBNs.

If you want to distribute to physical bookstores, then

having your own ISBNs assigned to your own publishing imprint is a good idea. I have my own imprint at www.Curl UpPress.com and I do have my own ISBNs, but it's certainly not necessary and I published for years without them.

For more detail on ISBNs, check out this article from the Alliance of Independent Authors:
www.TheCreativePenn.com/isbn

1.9 HOW TO SELF-PUBLISH A PRINT BOOK

S ince most authors now use KDP Print for POD and the dashboard is similar for ebook publishing, most of the fields covered in chapter 1.5 are still relevant, so I will just cover the extra information you need here.

Ingram Spark and the other services are similar in terms of the fields you need to populate.

Interior type

Choose black & white or full color; then choose Paper Color white or cream.

I use black & white for my interior, cream paper for fiction and white for non-fiction.

Trim size

Choose your book size. Personally, I use 5 x 8 for my paper-back and hardback books and I use 6.14 x 9.21 for Large Print.

For hardbacks on Ingram Spark, you can choose case

laminate where the cover itself is hard (my usual choice), but you can also use dust jackets if you prefer.

This is also the place where you can download a template for the interior once you've chosen a size.

Submit your book interior

Upload your print-ready file here in PDF, .doc, .docx or .rtf format. Again, you might get errors here that need fixing. It's not a problem. Just re-upload the file.

Cover

You can choose a matte or glossy finish on your book.

I prefer matte, but you can always try both as a test and decide which you prefer. Some colors can be different depending on the cover you choose.

Submit cover

Upload the print-ready cover file or use the Cover Creator tool to build one yourself within KDP Print.

Distribution channels

On KDP Print, this is separated into two sections: Amazon and Expanded Distribution, which includes Libraries and Academic Institutions, Bookstores and Online Retailers.

If you choose to use both KDP Print *and* Ingram Spark, then only complete the top section of this page and use Ingram Spark for Expanded Distribution.

Pricing

Based on all the options you've chosen and the layout of your files, the calculated cost of printing will be displayed here.

Obviously, a 400 page, 6x9 full-color book will be more expensive than a 200 page, 5x8 black & white book.

You can then add the price you want to sell the book for, which gives you a calculated profit. I usually make $2 on a print book. If you want to make more money, then put the price up. It's your choice.

You can never lose money on KDP Print as they have no returns and all the costs are included here. If you use returns on Ingram Spark, you have the potential to owe money for printing at some point, so I don't allow returns. However, some authors use returns and higher discounting to sell more effectively into bookstores.

Description

This is the sales description or back blurb that you have previously used on your ebooks.

You also need to choose the BISAC category which helps categorise your books. Ingram Spark also has Thema codes and Regional codes which can help categorise your books even more, so complete all the fields that are appropriate.

Contains adult content

Select if applicable.

Large Print

Select if applicable.

Many indie authors do Large Print versions of their books now as this is an underserved market and it's easy to do a print-on-demand Large Print book. Vellum even has formatting options for it now.

Check out my recommendations for large print here: www.TheCreativePenn.com/large-print

Submit for publication

Once this is all done, submit your files for review.

The POD services will email you within 24 hours with any issues. You may get a notification of some errors in the process. If there are problems, you'll be told what they are e.g. image is outside the margin. Fix the file and re-upload as necessary.

If you need to make subsequent changes to your books once they're live, remember that you can always upload new files.

Order a proof copy of your book or you can proof it online if you're confident enough to make it live in the stores.

If you're just starting out, then definitely order a proof copy. I'm established in my process now and trust my designer, so I just proof online and then order a copy once it's available for sale to put on my bookshelf at home so I can say, "I made this!"

1.10 WHAT IF YOU WANT HELP TO PUBLISH?

Some people find ebook and print book publishing too much of a hassle and would rather pay someone else to do it for them. That's fine and of course, it's up to you how much work you want to do yourself.

Publishing these days is not just a binary choice between traditional publishing with an advance vs. self-publishing and doing it all yourself. There are myriad options along the scale and lots of companies that can help you. Many of these companies are fantastic but some of them are sharks, so you need to be careful.

Spend a couple of dollars and save yourself thousands.

Buy *Choose The Best Self-Publishing Services* by the Alliance of Independent Authors, available on all the online stores. It's a guide to self-publishing services written by authors, for authors, with no vested interest in the companies described.

The Alliance also has a watchdog listing of companies and whether they are recommended or not: www.TheCreative Penn.com/watchdog

You can also join the Alliance and take advantage of the collective knowledge, as well as becoming part of a growing global community of indie authors. Check it out at: www. TheCreativePenn.com/alliance

I'm a Member and Advisor and I do monthly Advanced Self-Publishing sessions with the founder, Orna Ross on the ALLi podcast.

You can also check free information at the Writer Beware blog.

If you're considering a publishing company, do your research online.

Make sure that you know what you're getting into and what the costs are, not just to publish but also to make changes to your files over time.

Determine who owns the copyright and what control you have in the process. How much are the royalties and when are they paid?

You're likely to be excited about getting your book into the world right now, but you still want to be excited in the future. So, try to make publishing a business decision, not just an emotional one.

Recommendation: whitefox

You can use the resources above to investigate the many options for self-publishing partnership companies, but I get emails every day from authors who want a more specific answer.

I recommend **whitefox** for authors who want a premium self-publishing service with excellent attention to detail, quality printing, and expert guidance through the process from manuscript to publication and marketing. They are based in the UK and USA and specialize primarily in those markets.

Just go to www.TheCreativePenn.com/whitefox

I am an affiliate of **whitefox** so if you do use their services, I will receive a small percentage at no extra cost to you. I only recommend services I think are great for authors and **whitefox** do a great job for those writers who don't want to manage everything themselves and still want to retain the rights to their work.

1.11 HOW TO SELF-PUBLISH AN AUDIOBOOK

Audiobooks are the **fastest growing segment of the publishing market** and more opportunities arise every month for authors who want to get their books into audio format.

Streaming audio in smartphone apps means that it's easier than ever to buy and consume audiobooks and podcasts. Google Auto, Apple Carplay and Amazon Alexa make streaming audio in cars easy as well, boosting commuter listening. The Amazon Echo and other smart speakers have brought audio into the home.

Whispersync technology means that you can be reading on your phone or device at breakfast, then get in your car and continue listening where you stopped reading, and when you get home, cook dinner while listening again, all without losing your place. Amazon also bundles audiobooks with ebooks, and if a customer owns an ebook version, the audiobook is cheaper.

Listeners can get great value audio subscriptions with Audible, Kobo Audio, Scribd, Storytel and other services, plus library users can borrow audiobooks through local providers.

Most traditionally published authors have licensed their audiobook rights and many of those will never be turned into audio, so indies have the advantage of a faster response to this growing market.

The number of audiobooks available right now is considerably smaller than print or ebooks, so you have more of a chance of standing out. So, how do you get your book into audio?

ACX for Audible

ACX.com is the Audiobook Creation Exchange, where authors and rights holders can collaborate with narrators and producers to essentially self-publish audiobooks. It's an Amazon company and your book will be for sale on Amazon, Audible and iTunes.

At the time of writing, ACX.com is only available to authors in the US, UK, Canada and Ireland, but hopefully, they will expand to other territories over time and I'll refer to other options after this section.

If you are able to use ACX, the process works as follows:

The rights holder/author logs into ACX and claims their book

You can search with the Amazon ASIN, the number that Amazon assigns to every book on the store.

You have to legally own the rights to do this, for example, if you're an indie who hasn't signed a contract for the book or a traditionally published author who didn't license audio rights.

Enter in any extra details about the book that are relevant for narrators

For example, what type of voice would be best? An older African-American male vs. young adult female would be two extremes. You can also add information about reviews and sales, which is particularly important if you want to attract an experienced narrator.

Decide on the contract

The options are:

a) **pay the narrator an amount per finished audio hour** and you retain the entire royalty.

If you do this and then choose a non-exclusive contract, you can publish the audiobook wherever you like. This is now my preferred option when finding narrators on ACX as I like to go wide with my audiobook distribution.

b) do a **50:50% royalty split** with a narrator with no money upfront.

This can be a good way to get into audio if you don't have a budget, although this is only available for ACX exclusive contracts.

c) **record the audio separately**, either yourself or with an external narrator, then upload and retain the entire royalty.

I'm now doing this with my non-fiction, which I record locally and upload later.

Decide on whether you will go exclusive with ACX

If you go exclusive, you will get higher royalties, but you won't be able to sell outside the channels of Amazon,

Audible and iTunes. I choose to be non-exclusive so I can go wide with audio.

Upload an excerpt from your book for narrators to audition with

If you're looking for a narrator, you need to include a section that will reflect the book e.g. dialogue featuring the main character so you get a good sense of how the book will turn out.

Once you have loaded the book, narrators will be alerted to open options and some may audition for you.

When auditions come in, you can decide whether or not the narrator is what you're looking for.

You can decline auditions and give feedback if you want. If you're not getting any narrators auditioning, it's likely to be because your book doesn't have enough reviews or sales on it.

You can also find narrators through your author contacts and go looking for them instead of passively waiting. I actively found two of my narrators through recommendations from friends, and another found me through ACX.

When you find the right narrator, accept the audition, and then decide on dates for production

You'll need to QA the files, listening and checking the words as well as any audio issues. I trust my narrators as professionals and I consider the audiobook to be an adaptation, so I only correct obvious pronunciation issues which usually stem from British vs. American pronunciation or unusual place names.

Once the files are QA'd, the audiobook will go live. If

you're exclusive, you will receive some promo codes from ACX so you can get some early reviews on it, then you can start promoting.

Go wide with audio through Findaway Voices

If you are exclusive with ACX, your audiobook will only be available to those who listen on Audible and iTunes.

You're missing out on other global markets and companies which are expanding at an incredible rate like Storytel, Scribd, Kobo Audio and more, with new services emerging all the time.

You also miss out on library distribution if you're exclusive on ACX, and you can't sell direct or use a promotional service like Chirp from BookBub.

I use FindawayVoices.com to go wide with my audiobooks and I'm pulling all my books out of exclusivity when the contracts come up for renewal. I want my audio as well as my ebooks and print to be available in every market in every country. It is such an exciting time to be an author!

There are other companies that will help you get your books into audio and of course, you may choose to license your rights to an audiobook production company. Whatever you choose, make sure you understand where the audiobook will be distributed and how your royalties will work.

The money side of audio

If you do a royalty split deal with a narrator, there is no money paid upfront and you just split the royalties between you. ACX do this for you so the money is deposited into your bank account every month. You can also use Voices Share with Findaway Voices for this, too.

If you pay narrators upfront, which will usually be several hundred dollars per finished audio hour, you will receive all the royalties.

You can hire a studio and narrate the book yourself, or build your own home studio and record there as I do with my books now. There are some new skills to learn if you want to try this, but it can be creatively and financially rewarding.

Most authors with decent sales cover these upfront costs within the first year, and future sales will be profit.

If you retain the rights, then this can be a significant income stream over the long-term.

If you're traditionally published and have not licensed your audio rights, then consider working with a narrator to get your book into the world through audio.

For more detail on how to successfully self-publish audiobooks, check out *Audio for Authors: Audiobooks, Podcasting, and Voice Technologies.*

1.12 AFTER SELF-PUBLISHING

Congratulations! Your book is now for sale on the online stores, hopefully in ebook, print and maybe even audio formats.

There are a few things that you should do immediately and then we'll get into marketing in the next section.

(1) Buy a copy to check everything

You should always start by buying a copy of your book and checking it carefully.

If you do need to make obvious changes, it's a good idea to do that as soon as possible, before you start seriously marketing.

(2) Claim your book on Amazon Author Central

When you click on an author name on Amazon, you should be directed to an Author Page with their photo, list of books published, website details and social media info.

You can set up this page through Author Central at author.amazon.com

(3) Make a multi-link for Amazon

Amazon has a whole load of different stores and you want readers all over the world to be redirected to their specific store. You can set up one shareable redirection link with BookLinker.net.

You can also include your Amazon affiliate details, so you also make a few cents extra per sale. You can find out more on becoming an Amazon affiliate at Amazon Associates.

If you publish wide, you can also set up a multi-store link at www.Books2Read.com for your ebooks.

(4) Add all the buy links to your author site and online profiles

If you have an author website, you will want to set up a book page for your book and add in the buy links for each store once the book is available.

(5) Check out the sales reports for each platform

One of the best things about being an indie author is the control you have over the publishing process and also the transparency of reporting.

On all the stores, you can look at sales and revenue reports and see the impact of your marketing activities on your book sales over time. You'll also know how much your royalties will be, so you can reconcile them with payments later.

Kobo Writing Life even includes a global map so you can see which countries your book has sold in. As a travel junkie, I'm always checking that out and I'm up to 162 so far!

(6) Add your book to Goodreads

Goodreads.com is owned by Amazon, so eventually, your book will end up there through their automatic feeds, but you can also add it yourself manually.

No one knows for sure how much Goodreads data is incorporated into the Amazon algorithms, but they bought it for a reason, so it's always good to try and get reviews there as well as on the stores. You can set up an author profile on Goodreads and add information about you and your books.

1.13 HOW MUCH DOES IT COST TO SELF-PUBLISH?

I t's important to consider why you're self-publishing when considering the costs.

If this is a **lifetime goal**, then spending some money to make the book the best it can be is important.

If writing is your **hobby**, then consider how much money people spend on hobbies in general. Any hobby has some expenses associated with it.

If you are considering writing as a **career** and your book as part of a business model, then the costs are an **investment in creating an asset** that can put money in your pocket for the rest of your life and 50-70 years after you die according to copyright law. That is truly exciting, and I go into more detail in my book, *How to Make a Living with Your Writing*.

What are the main costs of self-publishing?

If you're doing this yourself without an author services company, as I do, the main costs for self-publishing are:

Editing

Most authors recommend using a professional editor to make your book the best it can be, but the cost will depend on the level of your writing, how long the book is, how much editing it needs and the editor you choose.

Range: $300 - $2000

In my experience, editing is more expensive at the beginning of your writing career as you are investing in becoming a better writer.

Lots more help and links to recommended editors here:
www.TheCreativePenn.com/editors

Book cover design

Most authors would also recommend paying a professional cover designer for a book cover. DIY just won't cut it in this competitive online environment.

Range: $50 - $300

Lots more help and links to designers here:
www.TheCreativePenn.com/bookcoverdesign

Formatting

Many authors do their own ebook and print book formatting in order to retain control, so this is often free or cheap if you're willing to spend the time upfront learning how to do it.

Range: $50 - $300

Links to formatting options and freelancers here:
www.TheCreativePenn.com/formatting

These are the main outgoings in order to get your book published as an ebook and print book.

Audiobooks will cost you around $200 per finished hour if you hire your own narrator, but this is a more advanced form of publication and most authors only move into audio once they have ebook and print formats sorted and a budget to take things further.

Publishing your book is free on all the ebook retailers and aggregators and also for print on KDP Print.

There are minor setup costs for Ingram Spark and Findaway Voices.

There will be other costs associated with marketing, e.g. building an author website, email list management, advertising and other activities you choose to do.

If you choose to use an author services company to help you do these tasks as described in chapter 1.10, it's likely to cost a lot more, so weigh up what your goals are and what you're willing to learn to do yourself before you commit.

1.14 HOW DO YOU GET PAID WHEN YOU SELF-PUBLISH?

I 've been self-publishing for years now, but it still gives me a real thrill to get my royalty payments!

It can be hard to imagine when you're just starting out, but many authors are now making good money from their self-published books. Some make enough for a nice dinner every month, others are running six and seven-figure businesses based on book sales, with every variation in between.

So how does the money work as a self-published author?

Check the various platform Help pages for up-to-date terms and conditions but basically, they all work in a similar way.

It's (mostly) free to put your book up for sale. The retailer takes a percentage of sale.

Amazon offers a 70% royalty to authors when pricing ebooks between $2.99 - $9.99 and 35% outside that range or for specific regions if the book isn't in KDP Select.

Kobo and Apple Books offer 70%, Nook 60%, and aggregators like Draft2Digital, PublishDrive, Streetlib and Smashwords around 60-85%.

Most platforms are free to publish but IngramSpark and FindawayVoices have a small setup charge.

You will need to add your **bank details** into the various platforms. Many pay by direct bank deposit in the author's currency or by PayPal, Payoneer, or by check in some circumstances.

Most of the retailers pay monthly, 60 days after the end of the month of sales.

For example, you're paid at the end of October for sales in August, although some retailers have a longer payment cycle.

If you sell direct, the money is in your account on the same day or within a couple of days, depending on the platform.

Tax information

You will need to do a tax questionnaire on most platforms, all of which have help documentation.

Non-US citizens will need to complete a tax form in order to avoid a 30% withholding tax which will cut into your income severely. But this doesn't have to be a big deal.

Just follow this helpful advice page: www.kareninglis.wordpress.com/tax

Reconcile your payments to sales reports

Most of the sites produce reports daily or monthly.

You can check and download **reports** to reconcile your payments to individual sales so the whole process is transparent.

PART II

HOW TO MARKET A BOOK

2.1 MARKETING PRINCIPLES

I have another book, *How to Market a Book*, which goes into a lot more detail on book marketing, so this is just an overview, but will hopefully get you started.

In this section, we will look at marketing principles and prerequisites, the things that don't change even when tools and tactics shift over time. These principles apply regardless of the type of book you write.

(1) Change your attitude toward marketing

It's important up front to focus on attitude.

Many authors feel that marketing and sales are negative in some way, but that just makes the whole thing more difficult. Whether you have a traditional book deal or you're self-publishing, you will have to learn marketing if you want to make a decent level of sales. So, it's time to reframe what marketing is!

Marketing can be defined as **sharing what you love with people who will appreciate hearing about it.**

Marketing is NOT tweeting "buy my book" or accosting

readers in bookstores with copies of your novel. You should never be pushing anything to those who are not interested. Instead, try to get noticed by people who will love what you do.

For example, if you've written a book on gluten-free weight loss, it's likely that you have achieved success with gluten-free weight loss. You're trying to help people, so why wouldn't you want to spread the word about the book?

If you write fiction, you're likely a reader and you love to find new books to immerse yourself in. I certainly do! If you've written a great story in a genre that readers love, why would you ever be ashamed or embarrassed about promoting your books in an ethical way to fans of that genre?

Once you change your attitude in this way, the whole marketing landscape shifts because it's now a positive thing. You're sharing things you love and attracting like-minded people.

If you start enjoying marketing and make it part of your creative life, you'll find it works a whole lot better — and it might even be fun!

(2) Think about the reader

Writing is about you. Publishing is about the book. Marketing is about the reader.

When we write, we are in our own heads. We're thinking about ourselves.

But when we publish and market, we have to switch our heads around to the other side of the equation. Consider the person who consumes the product and what *they* want out of the experience.

This will help you with the words and images around

your book. If you use references that others may not under-stand, it's no wonder they don't try your book. But if you consider what emotional reaction a reader might have to the words and images you're using, you will be much more likely to sell copies.

(3) Own your own website. Own your own email list.

When you write a book, you need to have somewhere to direct people so they can find out information about you and what you write.

There are many options for building your home on the internet, but an important consideration is who owns the site you build on.

If you use a free site, it is owned by someone else, whereas if you pay for hosting, you control that site. You can back it up and make sure it is always available.

Because things change over time.

Some authors let their publisher build a website for them, but what if you move publishers?

Some authors just use a Facebook page, but what about when Facebook changes the rules (as they have done several times already)?

Some authors use a free website service, but if that company disappears, what happens to your site?

If you're serious about writing and selling books for the long-term, then consider building your own website and growing your own email list. These days, it's easy and cheap.

Once you have your home on the internet, you can do other things to sell your book, but at least you'll always have somewhere to send people.

Equally, it's important to **build your own email list of**

readers who like your books, because again, who knows what will happen in the future with the book retailers or the publishers you use?

If you have an email list of readers, you can always sell books on whatever the latest platform is.

I personally use and recommend ConvertKit, which has a simple interface and everything an author needs for email setup and growth.

Check out my tutorial on how to set up your email list here: www.TheCreativePenn.com/setup-email-list

(4) Metadata is marketing

Metadata is the information *about* your book, rather than the book itself. It includes title, sub-title, series title, sales description, keywords, categories and author bio.

Think of it as the information that helps the online retailers understand where your book fits in the ecosystem. With hundreds of thousands of books published each year, the online stores need a way for readers to find the books they might like. This metadata helps them do exactly that.

Eventually, as 'big data' processing power grows, the book itself may be metadata, but until then you have to find the best way to describe it using these other fields.

When you self-publish, you will need to enter this data into the distribution platforms in various fields. It's important to try to use the most effective metadata, so research the categories that best fit your book and use the full amount of space for your description.

This is marketing, as your effective use of these fields will aid your discoverability in an increasingly online shopping environment.

If you need help deciding on sub-categories to target on Amazon, check out the reports on K-lytics:
www.TheCreativePenn.com/genre

You can also use Publisher Rocket to identify categories and keywords:
www.TheCreativePenn.com/rocket

You can also check out my tutorial on how to use Publisher Rocket:
www.TheCreativePenn.com/rocket-tutorial

(5) Consider how you will get attention

In my experience, writers are a combination of massive ego and chronic self-doubt!

We oscillate between wanting to hide in our writing caves and be alone and shut everyone out so that we can just create, and wanting people to buy our books so that we can make a decent income. I experience these swings daily, and I expect you do, too!

More on this in my book: *The Successful Author Mindset*.

There are so many millions of books in the world and many more published every day, so authors need to be responsible for getting attention to their books for the long term.

But, as above, it doesn't need to be in any kind of scammy or sucky way.

In the olden days of marketing, the only options were traditional media – newspapers, TV, radio, magazines and live events – but now we have a whole range of online options. These can be more effective, as they are targeted to niche audiences and can be measured more easily.

Some examples of getting attention online include:

- Blogging/writing articles on your own site, guest blogging, or writing on sites like Medium
- Posts, images and videos on Twitter, Facebook and LinkedIn
- Paid advertising like Amazon, Facebook or BookBub Ads
- Instagram, Pinterest and other visual marketing social media
- YouTube, Vimeo, Twitch and other video platforms
- Podcasting on iTunes, Stitcher, SoundCloud and other audio platforms
- Free online webinars or summits
- Email blasts about your genre or niche, through your own list or a paid list like BookBub.com

There will always be new tools emerging over time, but sharing in text, video or audio format will remain as the fundamental ways in which people consume content.

I fully expect to be running online events or even my podcast in virtual reality in the next few years, or doing a virtual book launch in the Paris Catacombs one day, but the concept of getting attention won't change.

Of course, you don't need to blog or podcast or do videos or social media to sell books.

You can have a sustainable career as an author by using the books themselves as a way of getting attention.

You can use free books as a sampler, a bit like the cheese and wine tasting in the supermarket on a Friday night. This little taste of your work can lead people to the rest of your books. You can also publish short stories in magazines or online.

You can write and publish books more regularly and take advantage of the way the book retailers work, driving more readers to your books with a spike in the algorithms through paid advertising and other traffic sources (often called the 'rapid release' model).

You still need a way to connect with readers, e.g. an author email list, but you can focus on writing more books as a way to get attention as well as sales.

Once you have someone's attention, your aim will be to attract them onto your email list so you can begin a long-term relationship. Selling one book is always exciting, but ideally, you want that person to continue buying for as long as you're writing.

(6) Attraction marketing vs. paid advertising

Whichever way you want to attract attention, you will pay with either your time or your money.

I've built a multi-six-figure business based on content marketing, putting out blog posts, podcasts, videos and useful social media in my niche, all using free media tools.

But it has taken me many years, slowly growing my audience through word of mouth.

> For more on content marketing for fiction, in particular, check out my course at www.TheCreativePenn.com/learn

If you want to grow faster, and you have a budget, then it's worthwhile paying for advertising to reach people more quickly.

Examples of effective paid advertising for authors include Amazon Advertising and Facebook ads, as well as paid promotional email lists like BookBub and FreeBooksy. These sites change over time, but the principles remain the same. You are paying to reach a specific target market.

For more on paid advertising, check out Mark Dawson's Ads for Authors course:
www.TheCreativePenn.com/ads

Of course, you can use a combination of both options, and many authors do. But it's best to put together a strategy so you know where your focus is over time instead of jumping onto every new shiny object. It can be overwhelming to try and keep up with the latest thing!

Remember to keep building your email list so that you can continue to reach people every time you put a book out. It's not just about a single book launch, but an on-going relationship with readers over time in order to build a long-term career as an author.

(7) Generosity, social karma and co-opetition

Authors are not really competing with each other because we can never individually satisfy the voracious appetite of the reading public!

We are all competing against other forms of media like gaming, TV, films and social media, all of which vie for people's attention and take them away from reading books.

Even if they do buy your book, think about the experience from a reader's perspective. They've waited months for your new release and then they devour it in just a few days, maybe even hours. They want another one immediately, but they can't get it from you, unless you have a huge backlist waiting for them to read!

This is where generosity and co-opetition — co-oper-ating with your perceived competition — come into play. You can help each other, promote each other's books, do joint events together and more to keep readers reading in your niche.

I recommend promoting authors who write in the same genre or category as you, but don't necessarily expect them to promote you in return. This is social karma: If you give first, then you generally receive back, even if it's from a different source.

This attitude of generosity and social karma keeps us focused on the positive and happy side of being an author. It's terrible to be comparing yourself to others all the time or feeling jealous about someone else's book or film deal, so stay focused on the positive.

(8) Be authentic

The more you share on a personal level, the more people will get to know, like and trust you, then they are far more likely to want to buy your books.

Of course, you have to draw your personal line in the sand. I don't share my address, or pictures of my family. I know some authors who use codenames for their children so they can talk about being a parent while still protecting their children's privacy.

I share pictures of my travels and what I'm up to for research, and over time, I have become a lot more honest about what I like. It turns out that there will always be people who are as weird as you, and they might like your books!

For example, I'm a taphophile. I enjoy walking around graveyards and taking pictures. I like ossuaries and crypts as well as art history and cultural aspects of travel. I share pictures on Instagram @jfpennauthor.

When I share this tidbit with a live audience, I generally find about one third of the room share my love for graveyards. That might also be true for what you're into, so be authentic and you'll find people who enjoy the same things as you.

I share my love of travel on my blog and podcast at www. BooksAndTravel.page where I talk to authors about their travels and the inspiration for their books, as well as sharing my experiences and pictures.

These are just some ways I share my personal side while still marketing my books in an authentic way.

(9) Build your author brand

Branding is your promise to the reader. It's the words, images and emotions that surround your work and the way readers think of you.

You can see this demonstrated very clearly with book covers by genre. Go browse the romance section and then horror. Or go and look at Nora Roberts' website and then at Stephen King's. Or my own thriller site at www.JFPenn.com and then my site for authors at www.TheCreativePenn.com. You can easily see the difference in branding.

Many authors consider using a pseudonym when they write books that differ in terms of audience. That's certainly why I use J.F.Penn for my thrillers and Joanna Penn for my non-fiction, because they are separate audiences and I need separate brands.

You should already have some idea of the books and

authors that are comparative to your own. Have a look at their book covers and the color palette they use as well as their author websites. What words and images are used? What emotional resonance does their brand present? How does it make you feel as a reader? Now try to apply those principles to your own author brand.

(10) Book reviews are important

Yes, book reviews are still important ... but not the ones that you might be thinking of.

Many authors obsess over getting reviewed in traditional media, but this type of review is unlikely to get you many book sales even if you can get one.

The important reviews are those on the online bookstores and places like Goodreads. They provide:

- **Social proof** so browsing readers can decide whether or not they want to sample or buy.
- Data points that show the **algorithms** of the bookstore whether this book should be recommended. Of course, we don't know the exact way in which reviews are treated as part of the recommendation engines, but they certainly play some part.
- Evidence of **quality** that is used by the paid promotional services. For example, BookBub requires a certain number of reviews and a high average review rate before accepting a book for promotion.

Free books are the easiest to get reviews on, so if you're struggling to get started, put your book on a free promotion and then do some advertising to get downloads. You'll soon get reviews on it.

You can also give away review copies to your email list. This type of Advanced Reader Copy (ARC) is commonly used in the publishing industry and is now used by many authors, although we tend to give away ebook copies, rather than print. You can use BookFunnel to provide these files easily to readers for their preferred device.

You can also pitch book review bloggers. Google the name of the author or book that is similar to yours + book blogger e.g.

"James Patterson Alex Cross + book blogger"

That will return a list of blogs that have read and reviewed Alex Cross books. You can then email the reviewer with a personal pitch that indicates they might like your book as it is similar to Alex Cross.

Do your research on their site and never write "Dear Blogger." I get that type of pitch all the time and immediately delete the emails! Spend a few minutes and make a personal connection and you have a far better chance of success.

(11) Measure the success of your marketing

Unless you're measuring the results of a promotion, how do you know if it works?

Marketing should ultimately result in sales.

If you're self-published, you can measure this easily, as you get daily sales figures from the self-publishing platforms. You can also check your rankings on the stores and take screenshots before the promotion and after to check results.

This is why I prefer online marketing to traditional

media and PR. If you have a clickable link associated with your promotion, you can track results and you will know what works and what doesn't.

When I first started out, I had national TV, radio and newspaper coverage but it had no noticeable book sales impact. Compare that to paying for an advert on BookBub or emailing my list, and the resulting sales spike. It's obvious which is more effective if you measure promotion, rather than basing your opinion on assumptions.

(12) Think long term

There are spike marketing techniques, like paid advertising, which will raise your book sales and rankings for a short time. But if you want a sustainable career as an author, you will need to consider a longer-term approach to marketing.

As we go through some ideas in the next section, consider these questions:

- What is your personality like? Are you willing and happy to learn new skills?
- What can you commit to for the long term? What type of marketing fits into your lifestyle?

For example, I like taking pictures on my phone and always share images when I travel on social media. This is authentic marketing and easily integrated into my life. It's sharing something that I like and others will find interesting, too. It's not related directly to my books, but it's certainly a way that someone might stumble upon my profile and then dig further. Sharing pictures is fun for me and therefore sustainable over the long term. It's also free.

I also do a weekly podcast on The Creative Penn which

has turned into the backbone of my non-fiction marketing over the last ten years. I also have another podcast, Books And Travel, which feeds into my fiction. Anyone who listens to hundreds of episodes of a podcast will end up being a fan! I also enjoy doing audio so I know I can continue it for the long-term.

But clearly, you can't do everything. So, choose what works for you and commit to it for the long term, and you will build an audience and book sales in a sustainable manner.

2.2 HOW TO MARKET FICTION

Marketing fiction is different to marketing non-fiction. I have both types of books and two quite different author platforms, so I know this from experience!

Non-fiction solves a problem, educates or inspires and is generally easier to target because people are looking for something specific. The book retailers are search engines for readers who want to buy books, so if you're using a title that is also a keyword search term, you will get sales from that alone.

But with fiction, we're looking for readers who don't necessarily fit into an obvious grouping, so they are harder to target.

Fiction also competes with TV, films, gaming, going out for dinner with friends or family time. When people want entertainment, they have a myriad of choices and, somehow, we have to stand out.

Of course, you can get attention by winning a prize or being on the front table of a bookstore or getting a film or TV deal. But these things are not really in your control.

They are lightning strikes and you can't build an author business on luck. In this chapter, we'll look at things within your control so you are empowered to market your book.

Here are the marketing techniques that I've found to work for fiction, in particular.

(1) Write more books

Walk into a bookstore and you'll see some authors have a whole shelf. Authors with just one book are hard to find and it's the same for digital shelf-space.

Look at the most loved and top-selling authors and they all have a lot of books. One book is not enough to build a career as a fiction author if that is a goal of yours. So, don't obsess over that one book, consider it just the beginning, and get writing on the next one.

Of course, first-time authors don't want to hear this! I certainly didn't when I put my first book out. I've tried every single marketing tool possible and I still continue to experiment with new forms. But after 27 books, writing more books is what I personally keep coming back to as the best marketing tool and the best way to increase my income as a writer. Because every time a new book comes out, more readers discover the backlist. You also have another chance to 'break out'.

For example, I only recently discovered James Herbert, a horror writer who was huge back in the 1980s. I devoured a whole load of his books in a couple of weeks and loved them. They were new to me, so it didn't matter that some were 30 years old. His stories stand the test of time and that is the magic of fiction. You can write a book now and it can sell for the rest of your life and 50-70 years after you die.

James Herbert died in 2013, so his heirs and successors now have the benefit of my readership.

In addition, a survey by International Thriller Writers found that it takes three to four books for a reader to become a true fan. **One book is not enough to capture a reader's attention.** Even if a single book breaks out and becomes the 'must read' of a particular year, it doesn't mean that readers will buy the next book from that author. They may not even remember the author's name. But if you have three or four books that offer the same type of experience and if a reader reads them all, you are likely to have a fan who will actively look for your next book.

By producing new work, you will develop an audience over time as well as finding your 'voice' and increasing your self-confidence. You will become a better writer with every book, so the chances of readers loving your work will also increase.

Remember that you can experiment with different forms. Try short stories (up to 5000 words) or novellas (20,000 - 40,000 words) as well as novels (50,000 - 120,000 words, dependent on genre).

You can also put multiple books together in a boxset so that the reader gets a deal and you get an additional sale. There are so many possibilities in this digital world!

(2) Write in a series or tie the books together somehow

Existing customers will buy more books from an author if the new book promises the same experience as what you've delivered in previous books and especially if they are hooked by your character and your world. This is why series are so powerful.

As a reader, there are some authors I will pre-order from

because I love a particular series, even though I might not read the other books they have. I'm loyal to the series characters, even more than the author, because I want to know what happens next and I get an (almost) guaranteed experience.

If a reader discovers and loves your series when you release book five, they are likely to go back and buy the rest of them, which means more income for you and more satisfaction for the reader.

A series is also faster to write, as you don't have to reinvent the characters and the world, you just need to find your plot and start writing.

If you write literary fiction or just like writing standalone books, consider the themes that tie the books together and think of ways to encourage people to move between them.

(3) Paid advertising

Paid ads through Amazon, BookBub, Facebook and others like Freebooksy/BargainBooksy enable authors to target sub-genres, comparative authors, and even specific books.

These can be incredibly powerful for driving sales — but only if you spend time testing and honing your ad copy, images, and targeting. You'll also need a budget for the testing period and then ongoing investment for ad spend.

There are books and courses on using paid ads as well as communities on Facebook where you can discover the latest tips. These change regularly as the platforms shift, so it's worth investing time and a budget to get to grips with this option particularly if you are a data-minded author.

Remember, paid ads drive sales for as long as you keep paying for them but dry up when you stop. So definitely consider using them as one aspect of your marketing plan, but also build your email list and author platform so you are not wholly reliant on them for the long term.

For more on paid advertising, check out Mark Dawson's Ads for Authors course:
www.TheCreativePenn.com/ads

(4) Use free or permafree first in series

A Smashwords author survey found that series with free series starters made more money than series without a free first book.

Of course, it's pretty emotional for many authors to consider giving away their book for free, but you have to think of it from the reader's perspective. Why would they spend their money and time on an author they've never heard of when they can just buy the latest James Patterson and know the experience is guaranteed?

But what if they could try a free taste?

Think about your local supermarket at the weekends. There is always someone standing there with a plate of the latest cheese or snack to try. The retailer knows that if you try it and enjoy it, you might just buy the whole packet.

In a similar way, if you can hook a reader in that taster book, then they may go on and continue to read more in the series.

The process that many established fiction authors follow is:

(a) Write a series of at least three books and make the first book free.

You can make a book permanently free on Amazon by publishing it on the other platforms that allow free pricing, like Kobo, Draft2Digital or PublishDrive and then Amazon will price match it once you report the lower price.

> Note: If you are exclusive to KDP Select, then the permafree first in series is less effective because there are so many 'free' books in Select.
>
> Being in the program gives you enhanced visibility, so leave the book at $0.99 or $2.99 and use the Select promo options instead which include five days free.

(b) Promote your free first book in series

You can use email lists like BookBub and Freebooksy to get the book moving or use Facebook or Amazon Ads.

There are many different sites that you can use now for this type of paid promotion. Some are cheap but may not move any copies. Some are pretty expensive but may have the best return on investment. Test them out to see what works for your books. You generally need a good number of reviews to be accepted for many of the sites.

This promotion will result in many readers downloading your book, some of which **will go on to try other books in the series** as they are (hopefully) hooked on your writing.

(c) Offer something in the permafree book that attracts people to your email list.

I offer a free novella, *Day of the Vikings*, for people who sign up to my email list at www.JFPenn.com/free

I wrote the novella specifically to tie my two main series together in order to help people cross over between them. The story features Morgan Sierra from the ARKANE series and Blake Daniel, from the London Crime Thriller series, in an action-adventure thriller set in the British Museum, London. In this way, you're using your free book to build your list for future sales.

(d) Once people are on your email list, you can let them know about new releases and giveaways

I send out a monthly update with pictures and news about my books, plus giveaways and book recommendations that readers might enjoy in the same genre.

You can continue to promote your first book in the series, as fiction stands the test of time, and a book is always new to the reader who has just discovered it.

If you'd like to learn more about **automating your author marketing** with this method, check out the free webinar I did with Nick Stephenson:
www.TheCreativePenn.com/nickjo

(5) Build a street team

A 'street team' is made up of your super fans, the readers who are so keen for your books, they will devour your

Advanced Reader Copies and write reviews as well as spreading news about your launch to the world.

It's a slow process to build one, because you need to invite your existing readers and then create a subset of your email list over time.

I have my Pennfriends and an application form that I use to invite people onto it. I only open it up occasionally, so it's exclusive, and I've formed email relationships with the people in that group over time. They get advance ebook copies of new books as well as free audiobook codes, plus I will also do print giveaways and other special offers for them.

Once you have a street team, you can ask for their help in launches, especially around posting early reviews. This is how many authors get so many reviews in the first week of launch, and many of these readers will buy the book anyway to support you.

(6) Content marketing for fiction authors

I've been doing non-fiction content marketing for TheCreativePenn.com for years, producing articles, video and audio that help people with writing, publishing and book marketing. Providing quality content gets attention and over time, and it builds up your site as an authority which means you get organic traffic from Google search and other bloggers linking to you.

But it takes time to build and is most effective for non-fiction topics, as people are actively searching for answers to problems online.

Most readers don't go onto Google and search for "new post-apocalyptic fiction." They are more likely to search for that on the online bookstores or discover their next read through browsing the store.

However, you can do content marketing around the themes of your books and any personal interests that tangentially intersect with your fiction. This could include:

- Articles, audio or video about the research behind your books
- Interviews with other authors in your genre
- Lists of recommended books in a niche
- Interesting Pinterest boards or Instagram images (e.g. Bookstagrammers)
- Video book reviews (e.g. Booktubers)

The most effective use of content marketing as an author is to **focus on things that your audience will be interested in**, and that will depend on the genre you write. It also needs to be sustainable.

I have some content on my fiction author site, www. JFPenn.com but I also have a blog and podcast at www.Book sAndTravel.page which taps into the travel research behind my books and also enables me to indulge my curiosity by interviewing other authors.

Content marketing can work very well for fiction authors

John Green, YA author of *The Fault in Our Stars*, has a huge following on YouTube/vlogbrothers with over 3.1 million followers. It's clearly a lot of work (that he shares with his brother), but he has dedicated fans and his books are guaranteed bestsellers with this much of a fanbase.

In terms of audio, Scott Sigler is a great example of an

author who has podcasted his fiction for years and built up a dedicated following that way. He reads his books on his website every week as well as releasing paid audiobooks later on and has traditional publishing deals as well as self-publishing.

The fiction podcast, Welcome to NightVale, became such a hit that it was picked up for a book deal, and the rise in audio consumption does offer further opportunities for podcast fiction.

Content marketing with images can be really effective for fiction and I use Pinterest Boards for my books at Pinter est.com/jfpenn which I create as I'm writing. It's fun and develops a following over time.

It's worth using images on whichever social media plat-form you prefer, as statistics show that images are shared more and attract more attention than plain text. Think about your own behavior. If you're scrolling through your Facebook feed, you're more likely to stop for an image that catches your eye.

Content marketing is free, but it does take time, so you have to consider whether it's worth it for you.

If you have money but no time, then the paid promo-tional opportunities might suit you better. I like to combine both for a long-term approach.

If you'd like to know more, check out my *Content Marketing for Fiction* course: www.TheCreativePenn.com/learn

2.3 HOW TO MARKET NON-FICTION

I n my experience, non-fiction is much easier to market, because readers are specifically interested in a topic or they want the answer to a question.

It is also more profitable because many non-fiction authors have other parts to their business, either in person as a speaker, consultant, coach or other practitioner, or online with multi-media courses and affiliate marketing. The book is often a way to demonstrate expertise and build credibility or a lead generation tool for people to funnel through to their higher-priced products.

Here are some specific marketing techniques that I've found to work for non-fiction.

(1) Write books that people actually want and make them easy to find

We covered the importance of categories and keywords in chapter 1.1 earlier, but the easiest way to market a non-fiction book is to write books that people want in the first place!

- Research the categories and sub-categories where readers shop as they relate to your topic
- Use keyword-specific book titles and metadata
- Use covers that resonate with the genre and target market
- Make sure the sample of the book offers enough information so that they want to read more
- Write more books in the same niche so readers will buy more than one

You can also use a series in the same way that fiction authors do. Just use the series title field on the self-publishing platforms to link the books together.

(2) Build an email list and create a funnel

My own non-fiction funnel looks like this:

I have a website, TheCreativePenn.com that attracts people through content marketing (blog posts and a podcast). On the site, I offer a useful free Author Blueprint and a self-publishing mini-course that people can sign up for at www.TheCreativePenn.com/blueprint

They receive a series of emails, videos and audios that take them through the process of writing, publishing and marketing a book for free, but also contain links to my non-fiction books and affiliate links to products and services that I recommend.

My non-fiction books are on topics that my target market want to read, e.g. *How to Market a Book* and *How to Make a Living with Your Writing*, so that if people buy one, they might also want to read others as they relate to the specific niche.

If people find the books first, each one has a call to

action that points them at the Author Blueprint, so the funnel has multiple entry points.

Like many non-fiction authors, I also have higher-priced products. I have online courses at www.TheCreativePenn. com/learn as well as offering professional speaking, and if people find the free information or my books useful, they can transition to these higher levels.

(3) Use paid advertising

Many non-fiction authors up-sell higher price products within their books, for example, courses, consulting, and speaking, so paid ads can be significantly more profitable than for fiction authors.

Personally, I do a lot more paid advertising for my non-fiction books, even the free ones, than my fiction because of the potential for extra income. If you have a budget, it's definitely worth making paid ads part of your strategy.

As stated in the previous marketing fiction chapter, paid ads through Amazon, BookBub, Facebook and others like Freebooksy/BargainBooksy enable authors to target sub-genres, comparative authors, and even specific books.

These can be incredibly powerful for driving sales — but only if you spend time testing and honing your ad copy, images, and targeting. You'll also need a budget for the testing period and then ongoing investment for ad spend.

There are books and courses on using paid ads as well as communities on Facebook where you can discover the latest tips. These change regularly as the platforms shift, so it's worth investing time and a budget to get to grips with this option particularly if you are a data-minded author.

Remember, paid ads drive sales for as long as you keep paying for them but dry up when you stop. So definitely consider using them as one aspect of your marketing plan, but also build your email list and author platform so you are not wholly reliant on them for the long term.

For more on paid advertising, check out Mark Dawson's Ads for Authors course:
www.TheCreativePenn.com/ads

(4) Content marketing

If you want to build up a platform over time, where traffic eventually comes to you for free, then you can also build up content marketing that drives people to your email list and into your funnel as above.

Once you're clear on your niche and target audience as well as the keywords that relate to your book, you can use that information to create content that people will want and that will bring people to your books. You can also do it in advance of your book launch, so you have readers ready and waiting.

Some possibilities for non-fiction content marketing include:

Write more non-fiction books and vary the length

In the non-fiction niches, there are a lot of books that are quite short e.g. around 20,000 words. You can make one of these permanently free as a way into your funnel.

Podcast within your niche

Although podcasting takes time, it's a great way to build a loyal fanbase.

If you don't want to go as far as producing your own podcast, you can pitch podcasters to have you on as a guest. Make sure you're a good fit for the show by listening to a number of episodes in advance and pitching a specific topic that would be useful to the audience. This is my preferred medium and I have *The Creative Penn Podcast* as well as *Books And Travel*.

Produce videos

These can be interviews, tips or entertaining snippets. There are no rules!

Video is a great way to communicate and build trust because ultimately, we judge someone by their body language far more quickly than their words. If you enjoy video and can commit to regular production, it can be a fantastic form of content marketing.

Blog/write articles

This can be on your own site and/or guest post on more established sites or post them on Facebook, Medium, LinkedIn and other high-traffic sites.

Guest posting can be really effective for non-fiction book marketing, in particular, but only if you write for sites that specifically focus on your niche.

Image marketing

Consider sharing pictures or inspirational quotes from your book on social media. Certainly, all your content should have some kind of image attached, but some content marketers focus entirely on the image platforms like Pinterest or Instagram for the foundation of their business.

Is content marketing worth doing for non-fiction?

Is it worth building a platform?

For me, it's absolutely been worth it, as my multi-six-figure business is built on the back of my podcast and blog at The Creative Penn. I have a lot of information available for free, but I also have books and courses for those who want to take it further and plenty of affiliate products for multiple streams of income.

I travel the world as a professional speaker as a result of building my platform online and I love the work I do. I continue to blog, podcast, and share on social media because I still find value in it.

But you have to consider what you want for the long term and what effort you want to put in. Are you building a long-term business? Or is this all about one book for you?

What do you already enjoy in terms of content consumption? What would make sense for you to produce? For example, I listen to a lot of podcasts but rarely watch video, which is why I focus more on audio than video production.

If you want to be effective at content marketing, my quick tips would be:

Understand what your target market wants

Then dominate that niche by producing specific, high-quality content that will be relevant for the longer term.

Learn basic copywriting skills around headlines and how content is structured online

Writing a book is very different to writing a blog post that results in the reader taking action. Check out

www.copyblogger.com for great content on copywriting.

Be consistent

My podcast used to be ad hoc, but when I switched to a weekly show, the engagement and traffic really took off.

If you produce consistently, you will build book sales and your online platform over time. All I've done is write pretty much every day, podcast, blog and share regularly, and over the last decade, this process has built up to a significant online business. I recommend reading *The Compound Effect* by Darren Hardy, as it really brings home the idea of a little bit every day making a difference.

Be authentic

Share your personal journey and your ups and downs and people will resonate with that so much more than a stilted business-like persona.

Make sure you are always sharing your own spin on particular topics, don't just share other people's thoughts or reuse ideas. In the end, readers will connect with *your* personality and *your* voice.

Remember social karma

You should always be sharing other people's material more than your own. Give before you expect to receive. Use social media to connect with influencers and be useful to them before asking for anything in return.

These chapters are just a brief taster on marketing and of course, you can dive down deeper on every single one of these topics.

You can find more free information on marketing at www.TheCreativePenn.com/marketing or check out my book, *How to Market a Book.*

CONGRATULATIONS!

Now you know how to successfully self-publish and make a start on marketing your book. All you need to do now is take action!

I know self-publishing can seem daunting at first, but like any skill, once you've been through the process, it gets easier over time. It's also incredibly empowering to put your words out into the world and have complete control over all aspects of your book.

Remember, you can change things later if you want to – your cover, price, sales description, even the words in your book – so don't worry about getting things wrong. Just try your best, take it step-by-step and you'll get there in the end.

Self-publishing my first book changed my life.

Taking that initial step led me to leave my job a few years later and become a full-time indie author and creative entrepreneur.

It really is an incredible time to be an author. So, whatever your definition of success, I wish you all the best on your self-publishing journey!

NEED MORE HELP?

If you'd like more help in your journey to becoming a successful independent author, the following resources will help:

(1) Download your free Author Blueprint and mini course

This free ebook and mini-course will take you through writing fiction and non-fiction as well as self-publishing and book marketing.

www.TheCreativePenn.com/blueprint

(2) Listen to The Creative Penn free weekly podcast

Join me every Monday for The Creative Penn Podcast where I interview authors and professionals about writing, publishing, book marketing and creative entrepreneurship.

www.TheCreativePenn.com/podcast

(3) Check out my other Books for Authors

I have some other books that might help you, all available in print, ebook and most in audiobook formats on all the major bookstores.

www.TheCreativePenn.com/books
> You can also buy books directly from me in all formats
at www.CreativePennBooks.com

(4) Check out my Courses for Authors

If you'd like to take your learning even further, check out my courses for authors, including How to Write a Novel, How to Write Non-Fiction, Productivity for Authors, Content Marketing for Fiction, and more.

www.TheCreativePenn.com/learn

MORE BOOKS AND COURSES FROM JOANNA PENN

Non-Fiction Books for Authors

How to Write Non-Fiction
How to Write a Novel
How to Market a Book
How to Make a Living with Your Writing
Productivity for Authors
Successful Self-Publishing
Your Author Business Plan
The Successful Author Mindset
Public Speaking for Authors, Creatives and Other Introverts
Audio for Authors: Audiobooks, Podcasting, and Voice
Technologies
The Healthy Writer
Business for Authors: How to be an Author Entrepreneur
The Relaxed Author
Co-writing a Book
Career Change

Links to all the stores:
www.TheCreativePenn.com/books

Buy books directly from me in all formats at:
www.CreativePennBooks.com

Courses for authors

How to Write a Novel
How to Write Non-Fiction
Multiple Streams of Income from your Writing
Your Author Business Plan
Content Marketing for Fiction
Productivity for Authors
Turn What You Know Into An Online Course
Co-Writing a Book

www.TheCreativePenn.com/courses

Thriller novels as J.F.Penn

ARKANE Action-adventure Thrillers
Stone of Fire #1
Crypt of Bone #2
Ark of Blood #3
One Day In Budapest #4
Day of the Vikings #5
Gates of Hell #6
One Day in New York #7
Destroyer of Worlds #8
End of Days #9
Valley of Dry Bones #10

Tree of Life #11
Tomb of Relics #12

Brooke and Daniel Crime Thrillers
Desecration #1
Delirium #2
Deviance #3

Mapwalker Dark Fantasy Trilogy
Map of Shadows #1
Map of Plagues #2
Map of the Impossible #3

Other Books and Short Stories
Risen Gods

A Thousand Fiendish Angels: Short stories based on
Dante's Inferno
The Dark Queen: An Underwater Archaeology Short Story

More books coming soon.
You can sign up to be notified of new releases, giveaways
and pre-release specials - plus, get a free book!
www.JFPenn.com/free

ABOUT JOANNA PENN

Joanna Penn writes non-fiction for authors and is an award-nominated, New York Times and USA Today bestselling thriller author as J.F. Penn.

She's also an award-winning podcaster, creative entrepreneur, and international professional speaker. She lives in Bath, England with her husband and enjoys a nice G&T.

Joanna's award-winning site for writers, TheCreativePen n.com, helps people to write, publish and market their books through articles, audio, video and online products as well as live workshops.

Buy books directly from me in all formats:
www.CreativePennBooks.com

Love thrillers?
www.JFPenn.com
Love travel? Check out my Books and Travel podcast
www.BooksAndTravel.page

Connect with Joanna
www.TheCreativePenn.com
www.twitter.com/thecreativepenn
www.facebook.com/TheCreativePenn
www.Instagram.com/jfpennauthor
www.youtube.com/thecreativepenn

Printed in the USA
CPSIA information can be obtained
at www.ICGtesting.com
LVHW011627201223
766909LV00002B/272